My mother, Mary, shared a story with me.
It's a secret story that began in Nak'azdli Whut'en.
And now I'm going to share it with you in her words.

—Peggy Janicki

The Secret Pocket

Peggy Janicki

illustrated by **Carrielynn Victor**

ORCA BOOK PUBLISHERS

'Utsoo was kind and gentle. We spent many days at her house. 'Utsoo and 'Utsiyan had a beautiful smokehouse next to our lake, where meat and fish were smoked and dried for the winter. There was also a special rack for berries and maitlus. The fire had to be tended when the racks were filled, so 'Utsoo spent a lot of time there. She was not very big and was getting older.

'Utsoo had a pad by the fire to rest on, with pillows to pile
behind her back. She let me sit with her and just daydream.
We napped together too. Best of all were her hugs and how she
made me feel loved. It was a treat to get a sip of tea sweetened
with sugar because at our house, tea wasn't for kids.

That all changed at the end of summer.

My family was busy fishing at our lake. 'Uloo glowed with concentration while cutting the fish. I was four years old, and I was helping too. Which means I was playing with my brothers and sisters on the sunny, hot beach close by. That way our mothers, aunties and grandmothers could see us.

A large, fancy black car drove in. The driver was a priest, and the passenger was a nun. They came over to talk to 'Uloo and 'Uba.

The Sister looked at me and exclaimed, "Oh, Mary's perfect for our school!"

Soon after I was sent to the Lejac residential school, along with my sister Aggie and my brother James.

It was far, far away from home.

We had to live and sleep at the school.

Kindergarten began at five years old. I did not have a class because I was too young. I was allowed only to wander the hallways during class time. The other children would call to me, "Baby McKinnon, come visit us!" and I would go from class to class.

I was homesick for 'Uloo and 'Uba and 'Utsoo and 'Utsiyan every day.

It must have been even worse for my brother, James. He was on the boys' side of the school, so we never saw him. I would sneak glances at the boys' side, even though we were not allowed to look.

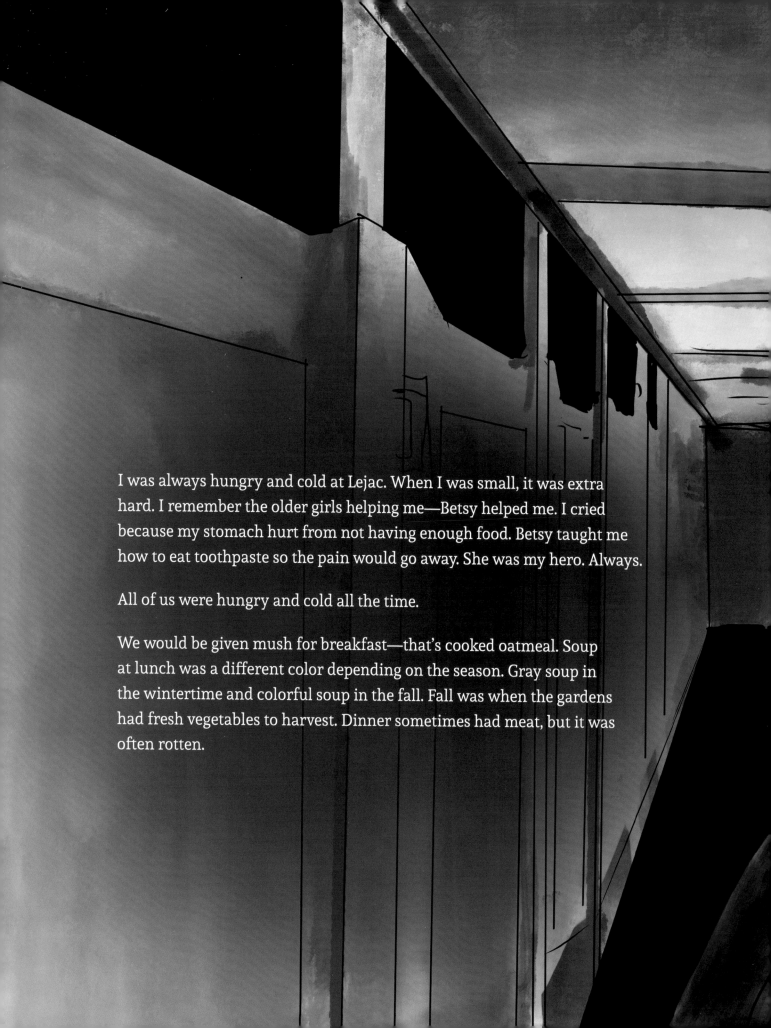

I was always hungry and cold at Lejac. When I was small, it was extra hard. I remember the older girls helping me—Betsy helped me. I cried because my stomach hurt from not having enough food. Betsy taught me how to eat toothpaste so the pain would go away. She was my hero. Always.

All of us were hungry and cold all the time.

We would be given mush for breakfast—that's cooked oatmeal. Soup at lunch was a different color depending on the season. Gray soup in the wintertime and colorful soup in the fall. Fall was when the gardens had fresh vegetables to harvest. Dinner sometimes had meat, but it was often rotten.

The Sisters were our teachers, and they were very strict, often cruel and had no sense of humor. One time my friend and I snuck down the hallway to see where they went when they left the classroom. Our eyes went wide with surprise when we peeked in the door—it was a bathroom!

We clapped our hands over our mouths and scurried quickly back to safety. We giggled for days.

Every year we spent fall, winter, spring and the beginning of summer at Lejac. I cannot count the number of days I looked out onto Fraser Lake with my heart breaking, wondering what 'Uloo and 'Uba and 'Utsoo and 'Utsiyan were doing. I was always homesick.

When we were home, we dreaded the end of summer because it meant that soon the gravel truck would drive into our community to take us back to Lejac.

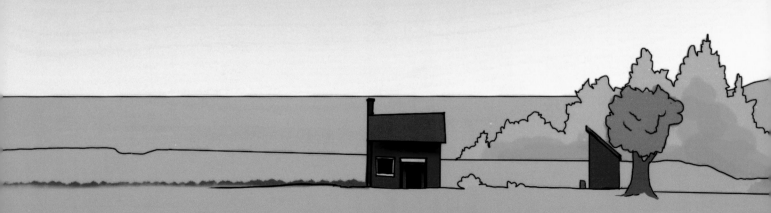

When I got older, I helped 'Uloo at home more and more. She taught me to mend clothing and sew moccasins together. We worked with small beads, and I always kept trying to match her skill.

At bath time I collected water from our lake and heated it on the woodstove. We poured the hot water into a large tub that we put in the bedroom. I was in charge of the littler ones, and I also watched for any visitors.

'Uba often sent my sister and me to fetch our horses from the distant pasture and get them ready.

When we were at home, we helped all the time, so I wondered how 'Uloo and 'Uba managed the rest of the year without us.

I remember one winter before the break when my heart overflowed with happiness. Children were getting picked up by their families to spend the holiday at home. Some families couldn't afford to travel to Lejac, because they didn't have enough time or money or supplies. That meant those children stayed at school for the break. I was getting very worried that my sister and brother and I would not be going home. Days passed, and no 'Uba. I knew it was easily a twelve-hour journey, which took time to prepare for, so anything could delay him.

I remember gazing out the window after a day spent vigorously scrubbing the floors for the pre-holiday cleaning and suddenly, very faintly, I heard sleigh bells!

'Uba's horses and sleigh came into view and
I was over the moon with joy.

Whenever I hear the song "Winter Wonderland," I remember the smell of lemon oil, the distant sleigh bells jingling on the horses coming over the snow, the cold of winter and my overwhelming feeling of relief, love and happiness. I was going home.

'Uba was Chief. He would visit us at Lejac to see how we were doing. The priest and nuns would only let him come if the visits were planned ahead of time. They would feed us good food in the days before he arrived so 'Uba would think we were being taken care of.

The Sisters would be cruel after his visit, making sure any extra food was taken away. We would go back to not having enough to eat. Also they would call me Chief-y to make fun of me.

It never hurt my feelings, though, because I loved 'Uba. I was proud of him.

All our movements at residential school were watched. In class, no elbows were allowed on desks. In the hallways and church, no talking was allowed.

Speaking Dakelh was forbidden.

The Sisters and Father were always watching and always ready to hit us with a leather strap.

One day I saw a classmate secretly holding something in the cup of her hand. I had questions. But I didn't ask what it was until the end of the day.

That's when I learned she had snuck into the kitchen, taken a tablespoon of peanut butter and hid it in her hand all day!

We found our ways to survive.

We made plans, especially for the top-secret missions to the kitchen.

We discovered that many of us could sneak food out. The hard part was moving under watchful eyes and not getting spotted.

So when we saw the rags in the rag box, we had a genius idea.

We sewed secret pockets into our petticoats to hide the food we took!

We secretly gathered all the materials—the rags, the thread and the needles.

We hid them until nighttime and then sewed our secret pockets in the dim light of our dormitory.

It was easy work because my 'Uloo, aunties and 'Utsoo were master sewers, beaders and kesgwut makers. They had taught us.

We woke up brave and hopeful the next morning.

Our hearts burst with pride when we walked past the Sisters with our secret pockets *filled* with food.

We sewed more pockets. We took more food—apples, carrots, pieces of bread. We fed the small hungry girls *and* ourselves.

We found our ways and filled our pockets with what we needed to carry on. We filled our pockets with so much more than food. We filled them with our future.

Now, as a great-grandmother, I look back at this time and see what sweet little geniuses we were. In the full face of genocide and cruelty, we secured our families' path for generations to come. We sewed our survival into every stitch. We come from a strong line of artists and geniuses, so we stitch with easy skill.

I continued my kesgwut-making, and my best friend, Josephine, taught me Salish weaving. Between the two, I was able to care for my family and conjure *pure magic*.

We were geniuses. We are geniuses. We will always be geniuses.

To all past, present and future matriarchs.
To my wee family, Chantel, Layla, Anthony and especially my
beloved Rick Joe, Snachailya for saying I should write a book!

Text copyright © Margaret "Peggy" Janicki 2023
Illustrations copyright © Carrielynn Victor 2023

Published in Canada and the United States in 2023 by Orca Book Publishers.
orcabook.com

Library and Archives Canada Cataloguing in Publication
Title: The secret pocket / Peggy Janicki ; Carrielynn Victor.
Names: Janicki, Peggy, author. | Victor, Carrielynn, 1982- illustrator.
Identifiers: Canadiana (print) 20220245916 | Canadiana (ebook) 20220246068 |
ISBN 9781459833722 (hardcover) | ISBN 9781459833739 (PDF) | ISBN 9781459833746 (EPUB)
Subjects: CSH: Indigenous peoples—Canada—Residential schools—Juvenile literature. |
CSH: Indigenous students—Canada—Social conditions—Juvenile literature. | LCGFT: Picture books.
Classification: LCC E96.5 .J36 2023 | DDC j371.829/97071—dc23

Library of Congress Control Number: 2022938343

Summary: This illustrated nonfiction picture book tells the true story of how a resilient group
of girls at a residential school sewed secret pockets into their clothes to hide food.

Orca Book Publishers is committed to reducing the consumption of nonrenewable resources in the
production of our books. We make every effort to use materials that support a sustainable future.

Orca Book Publishers gratefully acknowledges the support for its publishing programs provided
by the following agencies: the Government of Canada, the Canada Council for the Arts and the
Province of British Columbia through the BC Arts Council and the Book Publishing Tax Credit.

Artwork created through digital illustration.

Cover and interior artwork by Carrielynn Victor
Design by Dahlia Yuen
Edited by Kirstie Hudson

Printed and bound in Canada.

26 25 24 23 • 2 3 4 5